# Form

**The Scribbles Institute**™ *Young Artist Basics*

Published by The Child's World®
PO Box 326
Chanhassen, MN 55317-0326
800-599-READ
www.childsworld.com

Design and Production: The Creative Spark, San Juan Capistrano, CA
Series Editor: Elizabeth Sirimarco Budd

Photos:
© Corel Corporation: cover
© 2002 Estate of Alexander Archipenko/ Artists Rights Society (ARS), New York/David Heald©The Soloman R. Guggenheim Foundation, New York: 21
© Art Resource, NY: 8-9
© 2002 Artists Rights Society (ARS), New York/ADAGP, Paris/Tate Gallery, London/Art Resource, NY: 14
© David M. Budd Photography: 22
© Corel Corporation: 12, 25
© Giraudon/Art Resource, NY: 11
© Réunion des Musées Nationaux/Art Resource, NY: 27, 28
© Schalkwijk/Art Resource, NY: 30
Courtesy of the California Institute of Technology/National Aeronautics and Space Administration: 18-19
Courtesy of the Frank Lloyd Wright Archives, Scottsdale, AZ: 16

Library of Congress Cataloging-in-Publication Data
Court, Robert, 1956–
 Form / by Rob Court.
     p. cm. — (Young artists basics series)
Includes index.
Summary: Simple text and "Loopi the Fantastic Line" describe the concept of form in art and architecture.
  ISBN 1-56766-070-3
 1. Art—Philosophy—Juvenile literature. 2. Form (Aesthetics)—Juvenile literature. [1. Form (Art) 2. Form (Aesthetics)] I. Title. II. Series.
 N62 .C778 2002
 701'.8—dc21

# Form

Rob Court

The Child's World

Loopi is a line,
a fantastic line.

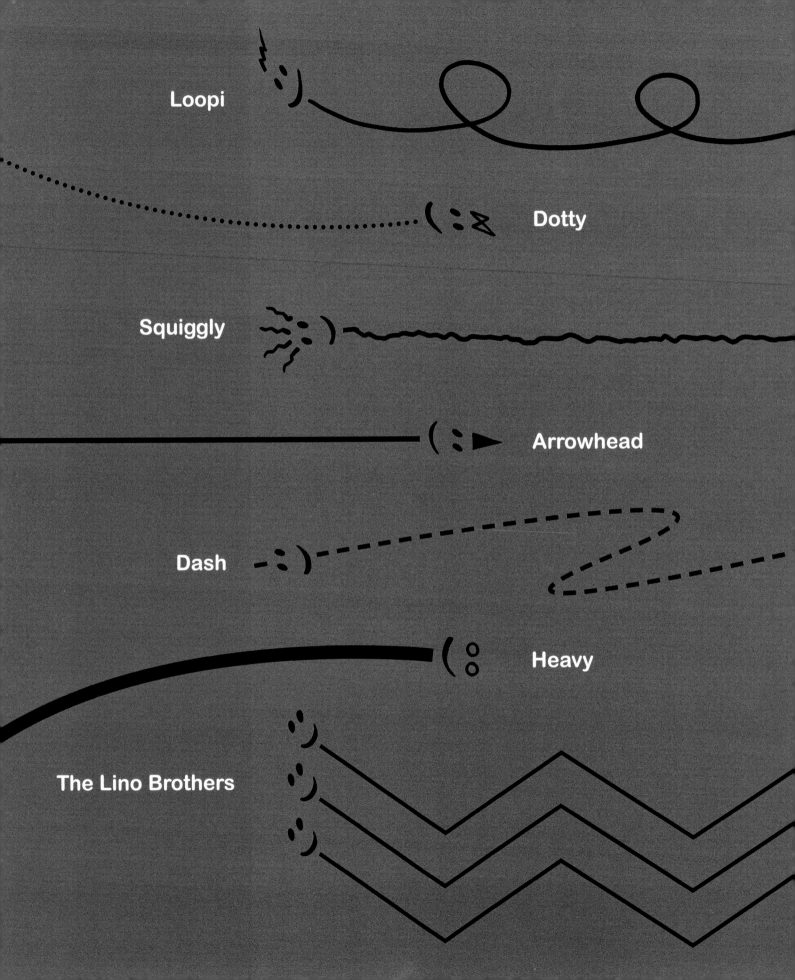

Loopi

Dotty

Squiggly

Arrowhead

Dash

Heavy

The Lino Brothers

There are many kinds of lines.

Some are dotted lines.

Some are squiggly lines.

Some lines point in a direction.

Some lines are drawn with dashes.

Other lines are very, very thick.

Sometimes lines work together
to help you learn about form.

For thousands of years, people have used lines to **represent** things. This cave painting of a running horse is more than 10,000 years old! It was painted on a flat stone wall.

Can you find Loopi in the cave painting? Loopi is a line that shows you the shape of the horse's body.

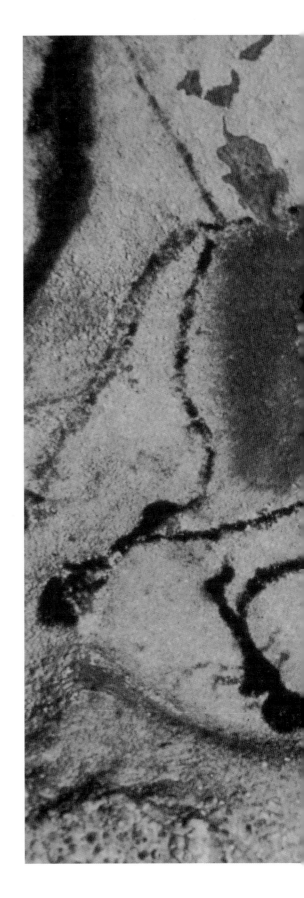

8

9

When lines and shapes are not flat, you can see their form.

The darker parts of this picture are the shadows. Shadows help you see the forms carved on this stone wall. If you could touch this artwork, how would it feel? Would it feel different from the horse on pages 8 and 9?

The wall carving in this picture was made by ancient Mayan artists in Mexico. The forms are part of a calendar. Dotty shows you the shape of a circle. Do you see forms in the picture that look like her?

11

This is a pyramid in Egypt. Its sides are made in the shape of a triangle. You can see more than one side of this pyramid, so you are seeing its form.

# The Form of a Pyramid

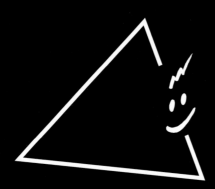

1. Loopi is showing you
the shape of a triangle.
It is flat.

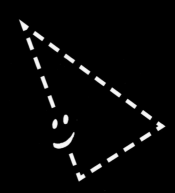

2. Dash shows you another triangle.
It is flat, too.

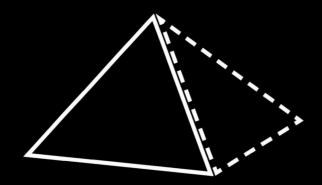

3. When you put the
two triangles together,
they make two sides of
a pyramid.

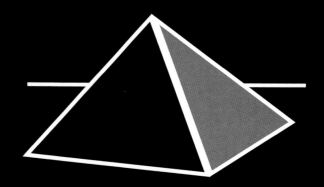

4. Now you see the form of
a pyramid. A horizontal line
behind it creates the ground.
Does the pyramid look flat?

Pol Bury, *16 Balls, 16 Cubes in 8 Rows*, 1966, Wood sculpture

Square and circle shapes are flat. Cubes and spheres are not. The form of a cube has sides. The form of a sphere is round.

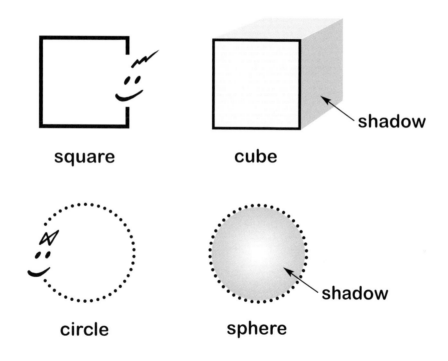

square          cube          shadow

circle          sphere          shadow

Shadows can help you see the forms. Artists create shadows in their work so that things look more as they do in the real world. Look at the picture at left. How many cubes do you see? How many spheres do you see?

**Frank Lloyd Wright, *Falling Water House,* 1935–1939.**

16

The house in this picture was designed by an **architect.** He used rectangles to make the sides of the house. The sides show the form of the house.

Above: Loopi shows you the shape of a rectangle. A rectangle is a shape that has two long sides and two short sides.

Left: Can you find Dotty in the picture of the house? She shows you a rectangle on one side of the house. Can you find other rectangles that create the form of the house?

There are many forms made by nature. Can you see natural forms in this picture?

Saturn is a planet in our solar system. It is a big sphere with rings around it. Imagine you are in a spaceship and could fly around Saturn.

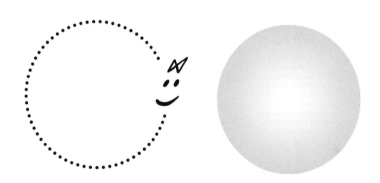

How is a circle different from a sphere? Why do you think the form of Saturn looks round?

Can you find Loopi in the picture of Saturn? Is Loopi a straight line or a curved line? Can you see the shadow behind Saturn?

A **sculpture** is not flat. It can stand by itself. If you could walk around this sculpture, you would see all of its sides. Can you see a form that looks like a person?

Do you see shapes and forms used in the sculpture? Do you see a sphere? Loopi shows you the shape of an oval. Can you find it on the sculpture? Can you name the colors used to create the sculpture?

**Alexander Archipenko,** *Carrousel Pierrot,* 1913. Painted plaster.

Sometimes you can hold form in your hands. The form of this pitcher is made to carry liquid. The form of its handle helps you pour the liquid.

The Lino Brothers show you the pitcher's curved form. Can you see the curved form that helps you hold the pitcher? Can you see the curved form where the liquid pours out?

You can climb on form, too!

It took millions of years for wind and rain to make these rock forms. They are a sculpture made by nature.

Squiggly helps you to see the form of the rocks. Can you see where the blue sky meets the rocks? Can you see other natural forms in the picture?

The artist Edgar Degas created this statue of a horse. It is made of a metal called bronze. Degas wanted to show the form of a walking horse.

Loopi helps you see the form of the horse. Can you see where the white space around the horse meets the edge of its metal form?

**Edgar Degas,** *Horse high-stepping,* **1865–1881. Bronze statuette.**

Edgar Degas, *Attendants and a Horse,* 1877–1880. Pencil on paper.

Edgar Degas drew this horse as an idea for a painting. He began his artwork by drawing **outlines** with a pencil. Then he drew shadows on the horse. The shadows help you to see the horse's form.

Loopi helps you see the outline of the horse's body. Can you see the outline of a person behind the horse? Can you see the outline of another horse?

How is this horse different from the one on page 27? How is it different from the horse on pages 8 and 9?

**Diego Rivera, detail from *Creation*, 1922–1923. Mural.**

Diego Rivera was an artist from Mexico. He made this **mural.** He used shadows to show the form of animals and plants.

30

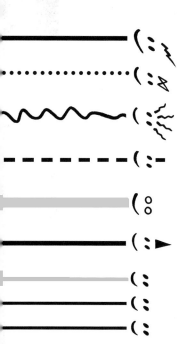

# Put It All Together

Look at Diego Rivera's mural. Can you see where he painted the jungle with dark colors? Can you see lighter colors where the sun is shining?

## Make a Painting of Your Favorite Animals

You can make a painting that shows the form of animals and plants. Start with an idea. Do you remember how the artist Degas made a pencil drawing of a horse? He started with an outline of the horse's body. Look at page 28 if you need help. Try to add shadows to your artwork.

## Students, Teachers, and Parents

LOOPI the Fantastic Line™ is always waiting to help you learn more about drawing with form—at **www.scribblesinstitute.com**. You can get helpful ideas for your drawings at the Scribbles Institute™. It's a great place for students, teachers, and parents to find books, information, and tips about drawing. You can even get advice from a drawing coach!

**The Scribbles Institute**™

**SCRIBBLESINSTITUTE.COM**

# Glossary

**architect (AR-kih-tekt)**
An architect is a person who designs and makes plans for buildings.

**mural (MYUR-ull)**
A mural is a picture painted on a wall.

**outlines (OWT-lynz)**
Outlines are lines that show the shape of an object. A drawing done in outlines shows only an object's outer lines.

**represent (rep-reh-ZENT)**
To represent something means to show it in a picture. A drawing of a daisy represents the flower.

**sculpture (SKULP-cher)**
A sculpture is a work of art formed into a shape to represent something. Sculptures can be carved from stone or made from metal.

# Index

**About the Author**
Rob Court is a designer and illustrator. He has a studio in San Juan Capistrano, California. He started the Scribbles Institute™ to help people learn about the importance of drawing and creativity.

This book is dedicated to Jesse and Jasmine.